Retirement Strategies:

Seven Decisions that Determine Personal Success

Esther King

Legal & Disclaimer

Legal & Disclaimer

The information contained in this book is not designed to replace or take the place of any form of medicine or professional medical advice. The information in this book has been provided for educational and entertainment purposes only.

The information contained in this book has been compiled from sources deemed reliable, and it is accurate to the best of the Author's knowledge; however, the Author cannot guarantee its accuracy and validity and cannot be held liable for any errors or omissions. Changes are periodically made to this book. You must consult your doctor or get professional medical advice before using any of the suggested remedies, techniques, or information in this book.

Upon using the information contained in this book, you agree to hold harmless the Author from and against any damages, costs, and expenses, including any legal fees potentially resulting from the application of any of the information provided by this guide. This disclaimer applies to any damages or injury caused by the use and application, whether directly or indirectly, of any advice or information presented, whether for breach of contract, tort, negligence, personal injury, criminal intent, or under any other cause of action.

Table of Contents

Introduction

Retiring can be a huge decision that should not be taken lightly. Studies have shown that people who retire and then have to go back to work have higher rates of depression, more work accidents, and face trouble connecting with their coworkers.

We all have to pick and choose when is appropriate for us to retire, but there are some times that are better than others. Of course, if you are offered some sort of golden handshake or package deal, your situation may be a little different. You really have to look at your well-being: mentally, physically, emotionally, financially, and socially.

This book will delved into the decisions you will have to make, the choices you will face, and the plans you should start TODAY so that retiring will be an easier process that you can do before you spend the rest of your life in a nursing home.

Each chapter will focus on a different strategy you will need and will look at a different part of the retirement process. This isn't a one size fits all strategy, but it will pose some questions that you will have to find answers for in your own life. Take each chapter by itself and focus on that – overwhelming yourself with too many ideas or thoughts will only lead to headaches and fear about retirement.

After you retire, what happens then? In a bonus section of this book, we will help you figure out what is best to keep you of sound body AND mind and how you can leave a lasting mark on the planet before you go. It isn't all about going to the gym and baking cookies for the neighborhood kids.

If you are near retirement age, congratulations for making it this far! If you are looking ahead and trying to make the right decisions now so that your trip is easier, great job!

Let's get started on this journey toward retirement!

"Retirement is like a long vacation in Las Vegas. The goal is to enjoy it the fullest, but not so fully that you run out of money."

Jonathan Clements

Step 1: Get Started Early

Some people really want to get started in preparing for personal success in retirement at an early age. That's not necessarily a bad thing, but remember that saving too much and not living your life will make you want to retire at an earlier age, which can be counterproductive to what you really want and need.

However, to get started early, try some of these strategies:

20s

The best thing you can do for yourself in your twenties is to get a job that has benefits, a 401k or IRA, and keep your debt low. Nowadays, it is nearly impossible to get out of college without debt, so make sure that you stay on top of those payments. Student loans never go away, no matter what you do, so you need to plan accordingly.

If you can live with your parents in your twenties, do it. Not only will it save you money, but it will also give you life skills and cement your relationships. Just make sure you aren't relying on them for everything. You want to use your 20s to establish credit so that you can get loans.

30s

Your thirties come quickly, and this is the time when you might start spending a lot of money: you are getting a house, a family, and money goes quickly. Your best bet is to once again, keep costs low. Try to live with less or cut back in certain places. Pay your home as quickly as you can, many people are still paying a mortgage when they look to retire, and that extra $1200 a month will look really good when you're 65.

In your early to mid-thirties, you should also try to move up the ladder at your place of employment. Not only will this bring in more money for you to save, but it will often come with a better retirement package.

There is one other thing you should do in your thirties that not many people will tell you: marry well. Don't marry someone who isn't going to get a career that will offer them the same benefits that you have. When the time comes, you will be thankful that you have someone who worked and has their own savings.

40s

By the time your forties come around, you should have quite a bit saved up already. Keep building! If you are making enough to be comfortable and don't quite spend as much as you used to, pay a little more on your mortgage or credit card bills every month. If you have that taken care of, take a little and invest it into the stock market. Those dividends might not pay a lot, but they will help.

Start putting the max amount of money into your 401k, or at least the amount that your employer will match. This will quickly build up what you have and take you to the next level.

50s

By the time you are in your fifties, you should try to eliminate all debt. Make sure your credit card is paid at the end of the month, you own your house, and you own your car.

Retirement is eminent in your fifties, and you need to basically put everything you can toward your retirement fund. Now is not the time to panic or go through your midlife crisis.

Now is the right time to start looking into your options, talking with an advisor, and having discussions at home. If your children are in college, you will have to figure out how you are going to help them, if you are going to at all.

While doing all of this won't ensure that you'll have the easiest retirement process of all time, it will definitely make it a lot easier. It's unfortunate, but the ease of your retirement comes down to the almighty dollar.

Remember that retirement isn't something that all of your money needs to go towards – you need to enjoy your life now as well. Take the time to enjoy everything as you go along the way. You never know what the future has to offer. If you want to do something, do it, but don't blow all of your money on things that you don't really need.

"Don't simply retire from something; have something to retire to."

Harry Emerson Fosdick

Step 2: What Do You Need to Live?

After you have saved up a significant amount of money, you need to start thinking about how you are going to spend that money. While it is great to think that we will be able to live on our pension, that probably isn't an option.

Realistically, pensions are only getting smaller and smaller, meaning that we will need to dip into our savings. Still, you should know how much you are going to need, approximately, each month before you take any sort of retirement package.

Now, this will all depend on how you live, where you live, and what you want to do. Obviously, retiring somewhere like New York City will cost you more than retiring to a small town somewhere. Will you keep your own place or will you go into an old age community? How much will that cost? Money isn't something we can objectively give amounts to: you will need to do the legwork here and figure out what exactly you need.

Bills

Your first stop should be your own bill cabinet – you will still need to do things like eat, watch television, go on the internet, drive your car, use your cell phone, and take a shower. All of these things add up very quickly, and they will take away from your bottom line. If you are still paying school debt or your mortgage, it adds up even more quickly.

Take out a sheet of paper and start writing down what your bills are today. Do you think you can cut your energy use or lower your car insurance? Start calling around to find out. Now, take how much money you are going to bring in each month. Is there anything left?

Remember that this is retirement, and you will want to have fun and go out and celebrate your success! You will need a few dollars at the end of the week to enjoy your life. Plus, you will be getting (if you don't already have) grandchildren, and they can cost a lot of money – but more on that later.

Health

Realistically, how is your health? Health insurance is expensive, and with most people looking to retire before they qualify for Medicare or Medicaid, it is definitely a problem. Will you be able to scrape by with the bottom of the barrel in terms of insurance, or will you have to get premium levels? You don't want to sell yourself short, as you will most likely need your insurance more and more as you age.

Take a look at how much that will cost you, and then start shopping around today. You might be able to find yourself a deal and save a few bucks.

Family

A lot of the money you spend will be for members of your family. If you started having children earlier, the chances are that they will be out of the house sooner, which can either positively or negatively impact your savings. If your kids pay rent, then you will be losing out on money, but you will also save on things like utilities and food. You will need to do some pretty serious algebra to figure out how much you will spend there.

Alternatively, you will want to start thinking about what you want to leave behind for your child. It's morbid to think about what will happen when you pass away, but it is a reality. If you want to leave money to your children, then you might want to figure that into a budget as well.

But more on spending that money in the next section. For now, just see how much money you will need to survive each and every month.

"There is a whole new kind of life ahead, full of experiences just waiting to happen. Some call it "retirement." I call it bliss."

Betty Sullivan

Step 3: Do the Math

Now that you have figured out how much money is required to live, you will have to put your nose to grindstone and do some pretty deep digging. You can't do some of this alone, and you might even have to make an appointment with someone at your office.

Remember that numbers are one thing, but the way you feel will be another. You need to think about your mental and social well-being as well. Sure, you might save money if you don't join a group or take classes at your local college, but where will your heart and soul be at the end?

What income will you have?

When considering your income, there are a few things that you will need to think about. The first is obviously your pension: how much will you get? That number needs to be free from any taxes or fees that your job might hide from you.

You should also consider money that you will have coming in from stocks and bonds that have matured. This is slightly more difficult to come by, as you won't have the same number each month. Your best bet is to average together the last year of dividends and see what you get – and then lower that number slightly. It is better to have too much money than not enough, right?

If you have anything else – rental properties (or tenants in your own home), a craft business, your spouse's income, or inheritances you think you will get, you should also factor those in some way – but don't bank on them being there: life has a funny way of surprising you. You also shouldn't bank on winning the lottery – that probably won't happen for you.

What will you need?

Take the amount of money you will have as income, and then take the money that you figured out that you need in the last section and subtract them. Hopefully you will still have some money left over. That money is necessary for daily life.

Do you have a safety net?

Money in the bank, inheritances that you are definitely getting, extra properties, and stocks and bonds are considered by many to be safety nets to retirement. Life throws us curve balls all the time, and that means that sometimes we are left without a leg to stand on. However, there isn't always a way for us to get bailed out, so we need to help ourselves.

Make sure that you have a monetary safety net. While money won't solve everything, it will make getting to another conclusion a heck of a lot easier. Whether this is just a rainy day fund for an RV to travel the country or a back account with tens of thousands of dollars in case you need to buy a brand new house, having a little something is better than having nothing.

If you don't have a safety net, start creating one. Start putting your change in a jar at the end of the day and not taking it out. Over time, that money will add up to a few hundred or thousand dollars. While that doesn't sound like a lot, it can really add up over time to being quite a chunk of change. If you do that every day for twenty years, can you imagine what you will get?

Take Action: A few years before you retire, make a budget that is nearly identical to the one you will have when you do retire. Can you live on it? Will you be able to go out and have fun? If you can, then maybe you can retire. If not, maybe you should start thinking about other options.

"Retirement means doing whatever I want to do. It means choice."
Dianne Nahirny

Step 4: Where to go?

A lot of the success in retirement boils down to whether or not you plan to stay in your home. There are benefits and problems with doing any of the following options, and neither is necessarily better than the others. Instead, it depends on your physical situation, your monetary situation, and your family ties.

I'm Moving

If you plan on moving, let's just say to Florida, there are of course costs there. You will have to pay for several trips back and forth, you will have to pay for a new home, and there are all sorts of hidden costs included in moving.

If you are moving away from your family, you will also have to start thinking about what will happen as you age. You might not be able to drive yourself or take care of yourself. All of that means that you will have to get help, which costs quite a bit of money over time.

You should also think about travelling costs to go see your family and the money you will spend getting to know your new town – all of that is money well spent, but it is still money spent.

I'm Staying

If you are staying, you will definitely be saving money initially. However, as you age, your house will as well. This means that you will have to start paying for maintenance costs, repairs, and general things that you didn't even consider – things like refrigerators, heaters, and roofs.

You will also have to think about the same things: lawn care, in home care, driving, and even cleaning. Who will help you out if you can no longer help yourself? Hopefully you've given yourself enough time that you have a few decades before you worry about it, but those years will go fast.

If you stay, start making a list of things that you've always wanted to do around your hometown. This is a great place to start so that you will know how much money you will need for some of the fun things. Then start making your circle bigger so that you have more and more options for what you want to do.

I'm Going to a Nursing Home / Assisted Living

There are many mixed feelings about moving to a nursing home or a retirement community. Many people feel like they are the greatest thing that ever happened to them while others see it as a prison sentence.

However, the best nursing homes will feel more like a community than a prison. Even if it costs a little more money, think about your quality of life. Look for nursing homes that offer classes, workshops, trips, spas, whatever your heart desires and you think will make you comfortable upon retirement.

If you have no other choice but going into a nursing home because of your health, that is very, very expensive. Some nursing homes can cost up to $800 a day, meaning that you need to have that money paid to get any sort of care. Medicare and Medicaid will cover you if your money runs out, but not before depleting your bank account, taking your assets, and, in some states, they can even go after your family for any money you might have given to them.

We will get more into this in the next chapter.

Take Action: What you do here depends on what you want to do after you retire. Start looking around at the cost of real estate where you want to move, start fixing up your house while you still have a lot of money coming in, or start looking up the price of nursing homes now so that you will know what you are looking at.

Making these decisions once you already have retired will make each choice feel rushed and won't give you the chance to think through and really weigh the pros and cons of your choice. This isn't something that you should take lightly – in some cases, it is literally everything you have worked for.

"There's never enough time to do all the nothing you want."
Bill Watterson

Step 5: Health Care

We have touched on it in the last few chapters, but your biggest expense in your twilight years is going to be your health care. As we age, things in our body just start to go wrong, and it is sometimes nearly impossible to bring it back to a place where we won't need some sort of medication, therapy, or expensive doctors.

Your health is all that you have, and that definitely means that it should be something that you focus on. If you have over a million dollars in the bank, but can't walk around to go anywhere, is it all really worth it? Make sure that you spend the money to keep yourself moving. Remember that you can't take it with you when you go!

The biggest question you will have to answer is: how will I pay for my medical bills?

Government Help

The main two types of medical coverage you will be looking at are Medicare and Medicaid. They are both government-sponsored programs that have been specifically design to help older people cover healthcare costs. However, most people get a little confused about what they actually do.

Established in 1965 and funded by taxpayers, Medicare and Medicaid are actually very different. Medicare is specifically designed to cover the healthcare and medical costs for the elderly, while Medicaid is actually for those who are too poor to afford it on their own.

Let's break it down, because you might qualify for one or both:

Medicare

You know how a certain portion of your taxes go toward Social Security? That is to fund Medicare. Medicare is available to everyone in the U.S. that is 65 or older – there has been some talk about privatizing Medicare (Democrats) or making the age older (Republicans) but so far, nothing has happened to change it. Medicare is available to everyone, regardless of income. There are four parts to the Medicare program, including:

- Part A: Hospitalization coverage

- Part B: Medical insurance

- Part C: Privately purchased supplemental insurance that provides additional services

- Part D: Prescription drug coverage

Both hospitalization coverage and medical insurance are covered by those deductions from your payroll taxes. You will likely have to pay something out of pocket for Part C and Part D, though the rate is likely

Medicaid

Many people who start out on Medicare will end up on Medicaid because they simple didn't plan well for retirement. Medicaid is a federal and state that helps individuals who make or have a certain amount of money or less. Over half of the money comes from federal government, with the rest coming from the states. This means that you can't transfer Medicaid coverage from one state to the other – each state has their own entity.

There are strict requirements to who can and cannot get Medicaid. Medicaid recipients to have no more than a few thousand dollars in liquid assets to participate in the program. There are also income restrictions. For a state-by-state breakdown of eligibility requirements, you can look them up on the Medicaid website or talk to your job, which should have information about Medicaid and Medicare.

However, just making less than a certain amount of money isn't the only requirement or qualifications to getting Medicaid. The program also serves special groups including, pregnant women, children, caretakers of children, the disabled and the elderly.

Medicaid covers things that they deem "medically necessary," including:

- Hospitalization

- Doctor services

- Family planning

- Nursing services

- Laboratory services

- X-rays

- Medical and surgical dental services

- Clinic treatment

- Pediatric and family nurse practitioner services

- Midwife services

- Nursing facility services

- Home healthcare for people eligible for nursing facility services

- Screening, diagnosis and treatment services for persons under age 21

You may also be able to get other services, depending on your state, including prescription drug coverage, optometrist services, eyeglasses, medical transportation, physical therapy, prosthetic devices and dental services. People covered by Medicaid will typically pay nothing for these covered services.

Nursing Home

Of the two, Medicaid is the one that we use most often to pay for long term care, which is generally not covered by Medicare at all. The high cost of nursing homes depletes funding for so many elderly Americans that they end up qualifying for Medicaid and they pick up the slack.

Take Action: Start looking into Medicare and Medicaid today to see what you will qualify for and what you will need. You should know how much coverage you will need, but you should also know what you qualify for – especially if you think a nursing home is in your future.

Remember: if you retire when you are still healthy, there are many years ahead of you. Spend the money so that you won't have to become one of those older people who is in and out of the hospital for things they could have had fixed years ago.

"There is life after retirement, and it is BETTER."

Catherine Pulsifer

Step 6: Make a NEW Budget

So now you are ready to move forward and retire, right? Not so fast! While you have made the bare outline of a budget, it is time to officially make a budget that will help you see exactly what you'll need. It isn't going to be super easy, and you will probably need a few weeks to gather everything you'll need (because you'll have to call up a few agencies to get it).

However, the good part is that you acquired some of this information for each and every step above – now we are just putting it together in a way that is organized and controlled.

Here's how to create your retirement budget:

What You'll Need:

- A full calendar years' worth of bank account statements

- A full calendar years' worth of credit card statements

- A full calendar years' worth of stock statements

- At least two paystubs for you

- At least two paystubs for your spouse, if you have one

- At least 5 different colored highlighters or pens

- At least one year's tax return (must be the most recent year)

You will take all of these items to see where your money has been going, you will have to mark them up with highlighters, so it may help to copy them, just in case you mess up. You will be using the highlighters to group your expenses.

How Much Time Will It Take?

- It may take you a few weeks to gather the information that you need

- 1 hour to collate everything together

- 2 hours to create your retirement budget

Level of Difficulty:

- Easy, but don't try to multitask: give this your full attention.

Step 1:

- Make a full list of all of your fixed (annual, semi-annual, monthly, weekly, etc.) obligations. This will include all of your monthly bills. Remember to include things like insurance, health care, and costs that only occur in specific seasons.

- Make a list of your **essentials.** Essentials including: housing, clothing, food, transportation, health care, and hygiene products. These are the items that you will have to pay for, no matter what.

- Make a list of things that are not essential, but you would like to have them. Try to rank them by importance: cable, cell phone, gym memberships, subscriptions, internet, and trips that you frequently take.

When you think you are done with this category, take a walk around your house and think of all of the things that you might have missed. Check your cabinets, look at your day planner, and even take the list with you while you go to the store.

Step 2:

Talk to your doctor about your healthcare. You have already made decisions for yourself, but did you think about cataracts? Dentures? Think about dental, eye care, and hearing. Those expenses will go into your budget.

By talking to your doctor, you might be able to get a better idea about what is in your future. Weigh whether or not your gym membership will cost more than your health costs – maybe losing a few extra pounds will save you money in the long run.

Step 3:

Create a bucket list. Your bucket list says the things that you want to do before you "kick the bucket" or die. You are meant to enjoy your retirement, so make sure that you do!

Think about things like travelling, hobbies, sports, entertainment, and day trips. You will spend money doing these things, so you might as well work it into your budget.

Want to go spend a week in Disney World? Budget a few extra dollars each month, and then don't use them as you save up for your trip. It is all about being cautious and planning ahead.

Step 4:

Talk to someone that has already retired. By talking to someone who is where you want to be, you will be able to realize thing you missed, get a new perspective, and face the realities. Maybe you can even talk to a few people. That will make your budget more realistic.

If you aren't comfortable with someone seeing your income or your bank account, create some fake numbers that are directly proportional (but lower) than what you are really planning for. Tell the person that you changed the numbers, and you are much more likely to get a realistic reading on your plan.

There are also professionals that you can go to that will look at your budget, including, sometimes, people in you bank.

Step 5:

Talk to your family. Though this is your decision, it also directly impacts your family. Do you want to be able to travel to see your grandson graduate from college? Maybe you can't take that expensive golf trip then. Begin to think about changes you may be willing to make that would reallocate money from items that are less important to items that are more important.

Your discussion should also include your spouse. It doesn't matter if he or she isn't retiring or has already retired, that person will be directly impacted by your decision to retire.

If you can, putting a little something extra into the budget for that special someone as well.

Step 6:

Your final job is to add everything up:

1. Total up all of your expenses.

2. Total all your fixed expenses separately.

3. Divide your fixed expenses into your total expenses.

How much of your income during retirement will go toward your fixed expenses? Does this align with your thoughts in Step 4 on how you want to spend your time in retirement? If not, you may have to rethink some things or rework your savings.

If you want to have more fun and lower your fixed expenses, you will have to start thinking of some ways. If you retire and your spouse is already retired, will you need two cars? Will you eat as much if you aren't doing as much? Find some little ways to lower fixed expenses so that you can have more flex to spend on the hobbies and interests you most enjoy! It is your retirement after all!

Chapter 7: Staying Active After Retirement

One of the most important things you can to after you have ended your career is stay active so that you can be healthy in both your mind and your body. Not only do you want to stay healthy so that you can spend all of that money you saved, but also so that you can enjoy life when you actually have time to be present.

Health issues are going to be a part of your retirement, but you do want to take as many steps as possible to keep it away. You want to be frugal, however, so here are six ways that you can stay active and happy without breaking your budget on expensive things:

Stay Active by Exercising

If you wish to get the most out of life, try to stay active in your body. Simply walking a few miles every day or playing a few rounds of golf a week is a good way to walk and have fun at the same time.

You can also join a gym that isn't all that expensive. If you are the kind of person that wants to be in a group, many colleges will have senior specials for gym memberships, and they will even help develop routines that will achieve your goals. Do some light cardio on your own with a stationary bicycle or by walking around the blog – or go to the gym and try the elliptical. You should also start a weight training program to keep you nice and strong. Keeping up your strength is the best way to prevent yourself from getting hurt if you do fall.

Get your husband or wife into it as well – or your grandkids! You will love all of the together time you have and you will both be healthier. Just make sure that you take it easy and remember that you are still "of a certain age" and can't do what you used to do!

Start Arts and Crafts

Many people think that knitting or sewing is such a stereotypical old person thing to do, but in reality there is a reason for it. Arthritis takes over the hands first, typically, and arts and crafts will keep your hands moving. It is also something that you will be able to do for a long time: exercising might not always be possible, but you should be able to knit for a long time.

Arts and crafts also give you something to leave behind: a blanket for your granddaughter, a dollhouse for your great granddaughter, and a handmade necklace for your daughter. Or, a great chair for your son, a keepsake box for your grandson, and a beautiful shirt for your nephew.

Do Your Own Landscaping

Landscaping can be quite expensive, and doing your own will save you a lot of money. Landscaping your own yard will keep you active longer, and it will get you out of the house. Maybe you will just cut grass, or maybe you can grow your own vegetables, or you could even try a whole new type of gardening! What really matters is that you are doing it all on your own.

If you live in a city and don't really have a yard, there are plenty of public gardens that are always looking for more volunteers. If you don't have that, you could always get yourself some pots for a window or your living room. Let your imagination guide you!

Doing your own landscaping saves you money, gives you exercise, takes some of the weight off of your family, and will keep you moving for a longer amount of time – plus isn't it great to know that you can take care of yourself?

Learn a New Language

One of the best things that you can do when you are aging, especially if things like Alzheimer's and Dementia run in your family, is to keep your mind active. Learning a new language teaches you how to create connections in your mind that you might not have learned before. It will also help you communicate with other people, especially if you live in an area that has a large group of people who speak a specific language.

This can be an easy and cheap activity as well. Many towns have free classes for seniors, especially at community colleges, so you can just go in and take a few classes. You can also purchase something like Rosetta Stone to really get a leg up. Plus, you can't downplay the importance of the internet, where you can learn how to do just about anything.

Learning a new language doesn't only keep you mentally sharp, but it also allows you to connect with others on a deeper level, expand your horizons, learn a little bit about a new culture, and even challenge yourself in a new way. Who knows, maybe it will even lead to a special trip in the future?

Read More

Keeping with the idea of helping your mind as you age, reading is a great way to keep you in great mental health. Reading is perfect for those rainy days when you can't go out and about, but also for when you are feeling lonely. If you aren't always surrounded by people, reading will help you to feel a connection. It also will allow you to travel outside of your locality, especially if that isn't financially possible.

If you aren't a book reader, even going online and reading the news for a few hours will help you stay sharp and you will learn more about the world around you. It's all about keeping your mind stimulated!

If you don't have the money to buy a new book every week (because who does – books are getting expensive!) remember that there is this old fashioned thing called a library!

Travel Your Hometown

If you were working for most of your life, chances are that you didn't really get to enjoy your surroundings. Sure, travelling the world is great, but it isn't always financially or physically possible. Don't let that stop you from going out and having a good time!

Check out your local town and find the great things that lurk within. Call up the Sierra Club or visit their website, as they offer great outings for people of all ages that are fun and often free!

You can also check out your AAA, Rotary Club, library, and even your local high school! They are always looking for chaperones for events, and they are often covered! Use your imagination and you can learn about anything from how to make glass blown ornaments to how a bill becomes a law!

Volunteer

Volunteering is a great way to combine all of what we have already talked about on these lists. While volunteering might sound a lot like working after retirement, you will be happy that you feel needed again. If you aren't sure where you can volunteer, there are tons of places to check: Craigslist, church, local libraries, museums, nursing home bulletin boards, or local animal shelters. Just pick something you like and see if they need help!

Volunteering can open you up to many amazing opportunities that you might not have had before. You will get out of the house, help others, and make new friends. Something that many people miss after retirement is the social interaction and the feeling like they are a part of a team – don't worry about that here!

Though an active retirement where you are doing something other than sitting on your couch and watching television and eating chips is something that you should actively strive for, don't overdo it. Retirees often feel that unless they're perpetually on the run, time will catch up with them and they will quickly become one of those pod people that they always feared they would be.

The key to a good retirement that will last for more than a few years is to achieve a healthy balance between work, play, and rest – kind of just like when you were working all throughout your life! Remain active and moving, but understand your limitations and that you aren't quite the person that you used to be. That isn't something to be ashamed of – life catches up with all of us. Don't break a hip while trying to swing dance or climb a mountain and don't get jumped trying to volunteer in an especially bad part of town. You can benefit your lifestyle and your retirement plans by remaining active, but only if you approach it wisely and cautiously. Good luck!

"Best wishes on your retirement. Enjoy a rest that's overdue. Take pleasure in the finer things that are awaiting you."

-   Judith Wibberley

Conclusion

So now you have a lot of questions that you need to answer. Seem overwhelming? That's probably a good thing! It means that you will take each decision seriously. You probably have some paperwork to do, some math to figure out, and important conversations to have with your employer, your banker, and your family.

Remember that retirement doesn't have to be permanent. You can also get a part time job, pick up freelance work, or even substitute for your local school district. Retirement is the start of an amazing journey, not necessarily the end of your life.

Who knows what the future will hold for us. The government might surprise us and work out a way to help the older generations more than they have in the past. Maybe you will win the lottery. Maybe you will live to be 115. Maybe you will die tomorrow. Life is short, and if your heart is really telling you to retire, if you can't stand your job anymore, or if you just want a change of scenery, there is always something that you can do for yourself. There's no mile that is too far, and there is nothing that you can't do – just keep digging and see how you can get some help.

It also won't hurt to take good care of yourself in the meantime!

You've worked for years and years – go out and play with some of that hard earned money: just not too much of it, you should still follow your budget!

-- Esther King

Check Out Other Books

Lifestyle Of Minimalism: How To Turn Your Home To a Clutter Free and Enjoy With Less.

http://www.amazon.com/Lifestyle-Minimalism-Turn-Clutter-Enjoy-ebook/dp/B00WYSZRFY

www.ingramcontent.com/pod-product-compliance
Lightning Source LLC
Chambersburg PA
CBHW070233210526
45168CB00020B/2170